THROUGH A BLACK MOTHER'S EYES

Let Me Tell You What These Eyes Have Seen

Faye Brooks

Cover design by: K&T Graphic Designs
Edited by: Critique Editing Services

Dedication

To our ancestors who were brought to an unknown land to build a nation that has yet to recognize their worth. To all the resilient black mothers and fathers who have witnessed and endured the pain, the suffering, the hurt while raising their children against seemingly insurmountable odds. Mothers and fathers who have lifted up continuous prayers for their families, as they have navigated a maze of survival in a world filled with obstacles set up against them. To any and everyone who would like to have a deeper understanding of the experiences of black individuals and black families, both past and present.

Acknowledgements

Thank you to my family and friends who have encouraged me as I navigated this journey. It has not been easy as I second-guessed myself on completing this mission that I feel has been given to me. My prayer is that this book will inform, encourage, provide hope, compassion, and insight into the struggles and the triumphs of those who have been marginalized and neglected. It is my hope that the scriptural references will provide comfort to the comfortless and joy to the downtrodden.

Table of Contents

LET ME TELL YOU WHAT THESE EYES HAVE SEEN

LET ME TELL YOU WHAT
THESE EYES HAVE SEEN

Through these old failing eyes, I have seen Middle Passage Ocean waves cresting and falling, slowly and painfully separating me from my beloved, lush, and beautiful African homeland. Behemoth, menacing ships with enormous sails carrying vulgar, depraved slave traders herding me and my family on board like so much cattle.

Legions of Black men, women and children chained, stacked, and cramped in the hulls or bowels of rickety ships, rife with pain, disease, and death, inhaling the ungodly stench of bodily fluids, mixed with blood, sweat, vomit and tears. Slaves being force fed stale, insect infested, rotten, and vile food to sustain the "human cargo" for arrival to the new and uncharted land. Stopping along the jutting Atlantic coastlines at trading forts, castles or barracoons with slaves shackled by rusted iron manacles or ropes, waiting in fear to be bartered and sold to the highest bidders for transport across the Atlantic, to faraway and unknown places.

Arriving as skeletal frames, weak, emaciated, near death. That is, those who were not thrown overboard due to there not being enough food to sustain them all. With the cold-blooded slavers calculating the reimbursement by the insurance carriers for those losses.

LET ME TELL YOU WHAT THESE EYES HAVE SEEN

Monstrous, menacing sharks circling in the ocean below while trailing the storm-battered ships, patiently waiting, and anticipating the feast of carcasses of those poor souls who expired, those who succumbed to the nightmarish journey across the vast ocean. And those who waited patiently for opportunities to fling themselves overboard rather than accept a life of slavery, of bondage, of loss, of the unknown, often unwittingly taking other chained souls to a deep and cold death.

LET ME TELL YOU WHAT THESE EYES HAVE SEEN

Distraught, frantic mothers, inconsolable wailing daughters, sons, and grown men, starving, frightened, chained, emaciated, and stripped of their humanity. Human chattel roped together, piled up on slabs in the bowels of ships and transported across the massive ocean. Even nursing babies snatched from their mommas' breasts, separated FOREVER from their mothers.

Men and women lashed, beaten to their last breath as a warning to others not to resist. Cruel, heartless, and ruthless ship hands striking fear to keep the "cargo" in line. Sisters, daughters, mothers, sons, and fathers raped, mutilated, and abused by their captors, their oppressors.

LET ME TELL YOU WHAT THESE EYES HAVE SEEN

The arrival of the Dutch slave ships in Jamestown, Virginia in 1619 with 20 plus Africans, more than 400 years ago.

Stolen men, women and children cowering, frightened, cold, and naked on auction blocks in the middle of towns waiting to be sold to the highest bidder as men explored their bodies for signs of strength, prowess, and power while also searching for flaws, weaknesses, and defects.

Men pondering the price to bid for slaves to till their land, build their structures, create their enterprises, "…$400 for this one; $1200 for the stout 20-year-old 'buck'." Slaves enduring humiliating probes into their mouths, examining their teeth, their ears, their genitals, and other body cavities.

Tears flowing from the eyes of women, girls, and young men as the auctioneer rolls his calls off the tip of his snake-like tongue. Families separated, wailing, clutching, and clinging to each other as they are pulled apart, thrown into wagons never to be together again.

Little children lined up and sold to work in the big house or work on Massa's farmland. Distraught mommas being dragged by wagons as their children are driven away. A people stripped of everything, including their names, their heritage, their traditions, their pride and yes, even their memories.

4

LET ME TELL YOU WHAT THESE EYES HAVE SEEN

Black men and women toiling, laboring in tobacco and sugar cane fields doing back breaking work from sun-up till sun-down. Providing the free labor to build a new and fledgling nation. The old and young, males and females, strong and weak laboring in the scorching hot, muggy, and sun-drenched fields.

Bending, planting, and harvesting the cotton, corn, the beans, the tobacco, the wheat. Labor that built the foundation of America's greatness, America's great wealth. Slaves being fed only enough to sustain their bodies, to ensure their survival to work another day. Toiling for no compensation, no benefit, building the future UNITED STATES OF AMERICA. Then donning their identification badges with their names and occupations to be hired out at night to work in the towns for next to nothing if anything. Full grown Black men being called boy and chastised for looking white men in the eyes. Stripped of their meager clothing and tied to trees. Beaten with whips until flesh is ripped from their backs. Branded with hot irons to stake the massa's claim so that no other plantation massa would dare to claim them. Human beings treated like just another piece of property, like an old mule, a worn wagon, a saw, or a piece of land.

Old "mammies" slaving in the kitchens preparing meals that they and their children could not eat. Preparing the hams and the chickens in the large common ovens in the massa's kitchen while saving the discarded parts of the animals for her family's meals. The pig intestines (chitterlins), pig ears, feet, tails, snouts, or the chicken's gizzards, livers, backs, and feet for the meals in the slave quarters with their earthen floors, straw beds, mud-sealed logs, and shuttered windows.

LET ME TELL YOU WHAT THESE EYES HAVE SEEN
Men hunted down by dogs if they had the audacity to desire freedom, the audacity to have hope, mutilated and left in the fields to die or left to hang as mangled "strange fruit" from huge oak trees while unaware old black women walked by carrying heavy loads upon their heads. Walking to and from the cotton or tobacco fields to the big house.

LET ME TELL YOU WHAT THESE EYES HAVE SEEN
Black people singing, songs of pain, songs of inspiration, songs of hope and Freedom; songs like "Swing low, sweet chariot, coming for to carry me home." Singing of the sweet chariot of the Underground Railroad Coming "low" into the South to carry one to freedom, to carry one home.

Negro spirituals telling of living a life in "freedom land." "Sweet Canaan – the Promised Land." "Go Down Moses, way down in Egypt Land. Tell ol' Pharaoh to let my people go." Songs with directions, sharing instructions on how to escape, how to find safe houses. "Meet me by the old, gnarled oak tree on the left side of the river." Sorrowful songs passed down from generation to generation. And songs to uplift and inspire, "I've got a robe, you've got a robe all God's chillun' got a robe: when I get to heaven gonna put on my robe, gonna shout all over God's heaven."

Old women piecing together quilts with coded messages to hang on clothes lines giving directions to routes north, and directions to safe houses of the secretive Underground Railroad.

LET ME TELL YOU WHAT THESE EYES HAVE SEEN
Second class citizenship – black men counted in the Census as 3/5 of a man as codified in the Philadelphia Constitutional Convention of 1787, an immoral agreement between the North and the South to secure political power and control a fledgling nation.

Mulattoes, Quadroons, Octoroons – Devalued based on the amount of black blood running through their veins – Mulattos 1/2, Quadroon 1/4, Octoroon 1/8, all the while knowing that only one drop of Negro blood relegated one to being "less than human." A distinction designating a people as never good enough, never able to measure up, never a whole man or woman, and for some, that belief remains even today.

LET ME TELL YOU WHAT THESE EYES HAVE SEEN

After emancipation – ex-slaves taking the last names of their last slave owners, the last name of a well-known person or of an admired president or the last name based on their occupation, or maybe just taking the name of an object they saw on the side of the road as they left that plantation for the last time. Left as free men.

These eyes have seen the end of the Civil War and the passing of the 15th Amendment of the Constitution during the so-called Reconstruction era. A law giving voting rights to African American men, only to be followed by repressive rules and laws to prevent black men from voting. Laws that were rescinded, leading to the return to "white supremacy," after asinine rules were implemented requiring African American men to "guess the number of jellybeans in the jar," or the requirement of paying poll taxes or owning property, or passing literacy tests in order to be able to cast a vote, while the illiterate vestiges of slavery lingered. Repressive clauses stating that if a Black man's grandfather had not voted then they could not vote. I've seen the holding of all-white primaries, (referred to as "clubs") that prevented blacks from making their choices known, discriminatory purges, where black men would arrive at the polls to find that they were no longer registered to vote. I've seen the prevention of former prisoners from voting, even if the imprisonment was due to a minor infraction or a calculated trumped-up charge. And yes, I've seen violence, intimidation, and threats.

Many lost their property or their lives because they dared to try to vote.

HOWEVER, a people's hope was born only to be crushed again by discriminating Jim Crow Laws with "whites only" signs here, "colored only" signs there. Rigid rules of separation as blacks rode in the Jim Crow cars on trains, and the back of the buses; only able to see a movie from the balcony of the theater and enter from a door on the side. I have seen blacks made to order their food from the window outside when their own people were the cooks inside.

LET ME TELL YOU WHAT THESE EYES HAVE SEEN
I've seen the races separated by so-called separate but equal laws, still unfair and punitive. Black families terrorized by men in white sheets and hoods burning crosses in their yards and firebombing their homes and churches, killing little black girls dressed in their Sunday dresses and ruffled socks.

Practices like sharecropping, robbing the black man of the fruits of his labor due to immoral credit schemes coming due at harvest time. Black homes and towns destroyed because the black owners were prosperous. Destroyed many times based on false accusations of young black men accosting white women to "justify" these terrible acts. Few if any jobs, just closed doors in the faces of those seeking fairness.

LET ME TELL YOU WHAT THESE EYES HAVE SEEN

Second class educational opportunities with hand-me-down books and school supplies even used basketball shoes passed down from the "white schools" to those on the south side of town at "the colored school."

Doors slammed in the black faces of those seeking equality, all the while, black men fighting for this country in wars at home and in foreign lands. Sacrificing their lives for a freedom that they did not have at home.

Unemployed black men having to leave their families in order to secure public government assistance for the survival of their wives and children. Help not available if there is an "able-bodied black man" who is head of the household. Even if that black man has tried time and time and time again to find work with no success.

LET ME TELL YOU WHAT THESE EYES HAVE SEEN

Marching for freedom in the civil rights movement with women and men fired from their jobs as domestics, drivers, busboys, train porters and factory workers due to their choosing to march for their equal rights. Men, women, and children marching for civil rights and being slammed to the ground with powerful water hoses. Crying in loud voices, as dogs nipped at their bodies, "If not now, when?" The bombing of buses, homes and churches, the beating and jailing of freedom marchers, and the killing of others. I've seen the signing of the Civil Rights Act of 1964, an act that outlawed discrimination based on a person's race, color, religion, sex, or national origin. An act that banned segregation. I've seen the passing of the Voting Rights Act of 1965. An act that banned racial discrimination in voting practices only to see that act not renewed right now in modern times. I've seen many things…

BUT LET ME TELL YOU WHAT THESE EYES HAVE SEEN AND WHAT THEY ARE STILL SEEING TODAY!
Still unequal opportunities and injustice due to the level of melanin in our skin. Still Black men and women shot and killed by those who pledged to protect and to serve for circumstances that would not result in death for those who are not of color.

Still disproportionate sentences based on color and economic status. Still unequally funded schools based on zip codes. Still denial of voting rights and fair housing opportunities. Still the lack of opportunity to build wealth for ourselves and our children. Still schemes to deny people of color access to the American dream!

LET ME TELL YOU WHAT THESE EYES HAVE SEEN. STILL!

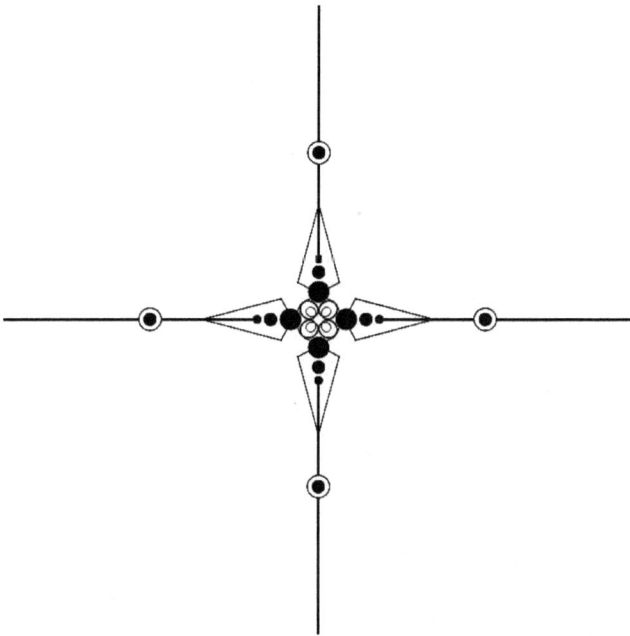

THESE
HANDS

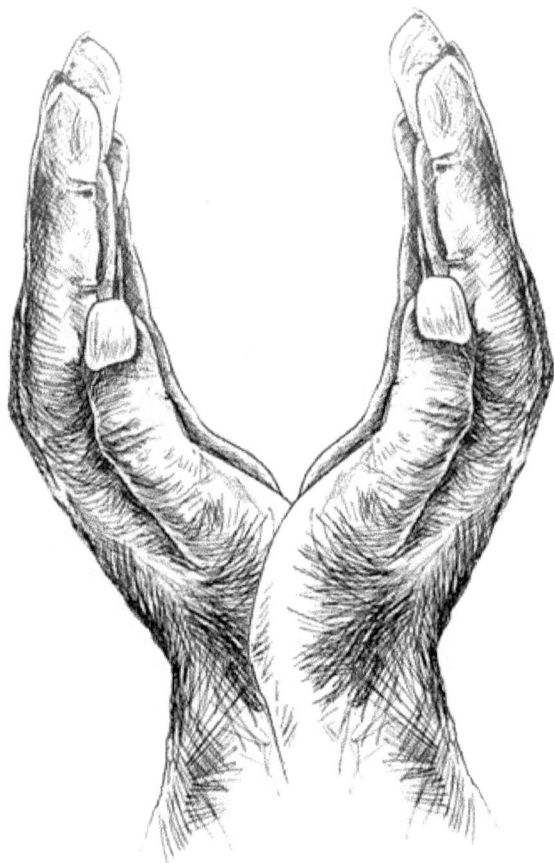

THESE HANDS

These hands have caressed my babies' heads

And cradled my mother's brow.

These hands have been my sister's stead

And explained to my brother how

We would survive, though days seemed dim.

With heart and hands, I explained to him

That our lives would be better, our days fulfilled

If we only stayed in God's Holy will.

These hands have known hardships, hurt and pain.

They have been chilled and drenched in freezing rain.

They have carried heavy loads in the stinging cold.

Have harvested fields with empty bolls

These hands have nestled to breast another's child

Longing to nurse their own all the while.

These hands have joined others in the struggle to overcome.

These hands have prayed that we someday would be one.

These hands have been shackled with lack of opportunity

Due to the dark hue of these hands you see.

These hands are tired of pressing on

But these hands realize that they must be strong.

For these hands must fill the space

Of those who have come before us of this dark hued race.

These hands cannot give up the struggle.

For these hands are a part of the chain

That links generations of people of color

That links 400 years of pain.

Each hand length throughout the generations

Has inched us closer to becoming a "whole nation."

My hands cannot break that chain

'Cause other hands remain.

Those living and those unborn

Must contribute to removal of these thorns.

Thorns of racism, envy, and hate.

So, hands be strong, a whole people's fate

Lies in your fingertips, in your touch.

Your link is so important, oh so much

But not just for us, but for future generations to come.

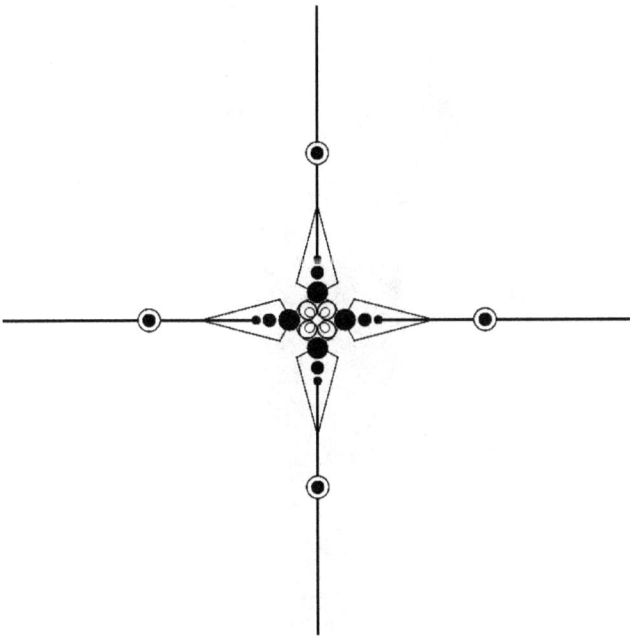

STAND

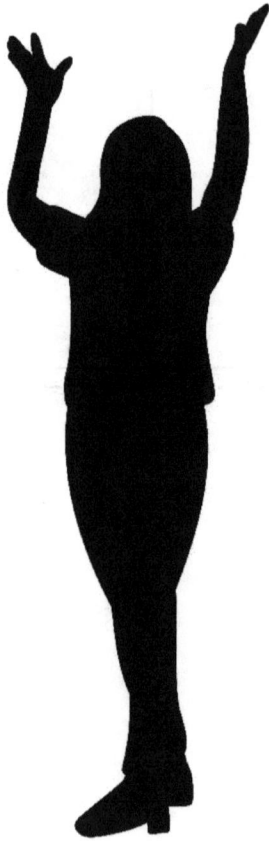

STAND

Like Joshua at the walls of Jericho
Marching seven times around
By the power of God and obedience
Made the walls come tumbling down.
Like Gideon
With his army of three hundred men
Up against an army of thousands
God tested his faith
And found him worthy
And the army of thousands ran!
Like Abraham
Leaving for an unknown land
Following directions from the Lord
For the promise of Canaan
On faith he stands
Faith and obedience to God's Word.
Like Noah's
building of the Ark
In the middle of dry land
Mocked and ridiculed by mankind
But on God's Word, he stands
YOU TOO MUST STAND!

THE
ANSWER

THE ANSWER

The vision was equality. Integration was never enough.

Even with integration, so many walls remained up.

Proud mommas sent their babies, their most valuable possessions

Into integrated schools with new textbooks, new lessons.

So, what went wrong; what was missing?

Stop for a minute. Reflect on the mission.

Just imagine being allowed to attend the grandest ball.

You go in your everyday attire as you enter the hall

Your shoes' soles have become unattached,

In your fingerless gloves, your dilapidated hat.

That old, ragged jacket with moth holes and stains

And shredded pants still damp from the rain.

But you walk in proudly. You stand tall and correct

You scan the room slowly, for people you have met.

But you are ignored, the tone has been set

And slowly but surely, you begin to fret.

Immediately you know you're not wanted there

As people point and start to stare

They don't know that your outside does not reflect who you are.

As you scan their expressions from afar

The stares of contempt, the looks of fear.

You struggle to integrate, that's why you're here.

You try to fit in, but each attempt meets disdain.

You ask, "Where is the host of this ball?" in a voice filled with pain.

"Surely he will support me." Soon you realize, you see.

He allowed me here because "this" was forced to be

But he ignores me and walks away.

Should I go or should I stay?

My psyche longs to feel welcome, but it does not come.

As I reminisce on corner gatherings with my friends and loved ones.

The joy felt being with each other, no matter our circumstance.

That sense of belonging was missing, but attending was worth the chance.

The pain ran deep, but it is just the start

For next comes the attack on my very heart.

Attacks on my mind, my heart were hurtful and rough

As I'm constantly told here that I'm not good enough.

With words but even more with deeds

I'm told that I am inferior and not equipped to lead.

"Your IQ does not measure up," they say

As I'm ignored and laughed at day after day.

Even the host makes me feel unwelcome, unwanted.

"Why don't you leave," they've often said.

I grow weary of this, but I cannot leave.

I will show them; I will make them grieve.

If by chance someone should speak to me

I will not answer, they will see

The taunts and stares now come from me.

I will fight back; I'll make them pay.

I'll start that immediately, this very day

I will just quit trying; that will get them too!

Now you're calling me hostile, and angry toward you.

And calling in the authorities to take me away.

To take me to juvenile jail for an indefinite stay.

When all I did was to rebel against the injustices I see

The killing of the very inside of me.

I did not want to be at this ball anyway

In the neighborhood we enjoyed each day.

We were all treated with respect, fairness, and pride

At this ball, you had to decide.

As in life you must do the same

Would you sacrifice, endure hurt and pain?

Was it worth all of that to stay? Many do.

And make it through.

But so many fall by the way.

The vision was equality.

As it still is today.

The struggle continues, but we must find a way

To break through these walls for our children's sake.

We cannot raise generation after generation of those who fall by the way.

Education's foundation we must lay.

Education is freedom! The vision was equality!

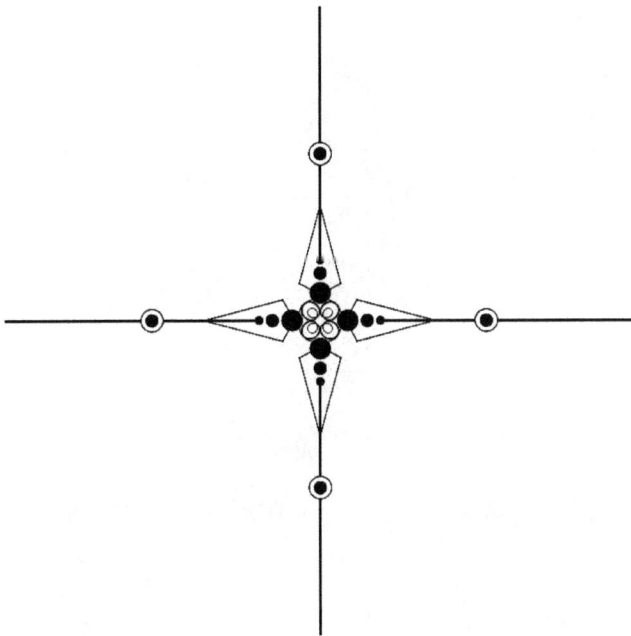

MY SON

MY SON

My beautiful black son

You don't understand.

I want you to live

To become a man.

Yes, it's true

That I hold on tight

But I'm aware of the dangers

To your young black life.

You're a precious endangered species

always in the line of fire.

From forces seen and unseen

Forces free and those for hire.

Yes, you wonder why I worry so

Why I keep up with your every move.

Well, I have seen more than you can ever know

Of pain that cannot be soothed.

'Cause the senseless killing of our sons

Over matters as simple as colors

And streets and corners to be won

Have cost the lives of many of your brothers.

And so, each time that you go out

I hit my knees to pray

That God will bring you safely home

To rise to see another day.

For so many sons have not made it home

So many mothers have cried.

For the souls of their boys, they continue to mourn

Because for "no reason" they died.

Why have people become so cold

And willing to take another's life?

Don't they realize that each body has a soul

That is destined for eternal life?

Eternal life in heaven or hell

The choice it must be made

In whose kingdom will your soul dwell

For God's kingdom – the price has been paid.

So, forgive me son if it seems

That I try too hard

To protect your life, to protect your dreams.

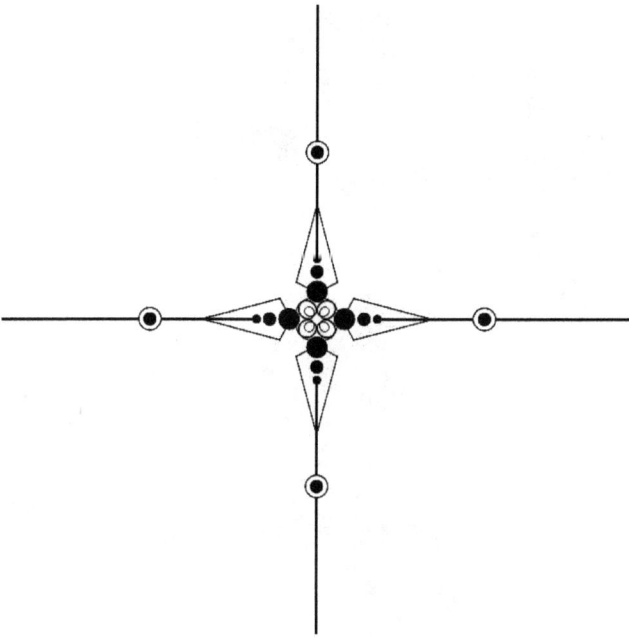

VULGARITY

VULGARITY

Child, what do you mean?

Are you on a mission? That's what it seems.

A mission to bring your brother down

With each flick of your tongue

On his heart you pound.

The words you speak

Each vulgar part

Seems designed to pierce his very heart

Why must you call your brother a M__F___

In your casual conversation

As you degrade him, you degrade mothers

Who are the backbone of this nation.

Why must that sister be called a B__t__h?

She is somebody's child.

Your words do nothing but dig a ditch

That should not be your style.

I fear you do this to impress

If so, you've been misled.

Your filthy tongue can only stress

The lack of knowledge in your head.

I believe if you knew a better way

To express your very feelings

Your tongue – those words would surely say

this vulgarity – you would not find appealing.

When you're spouting your vulgarity

Just what is it you're thinking?

That, this sista is impressed with me.

No – she thinks your words are stinking.

So, check yourself; do you really need

To make your mouth a sewer that seethes

Filth and vulgarities?

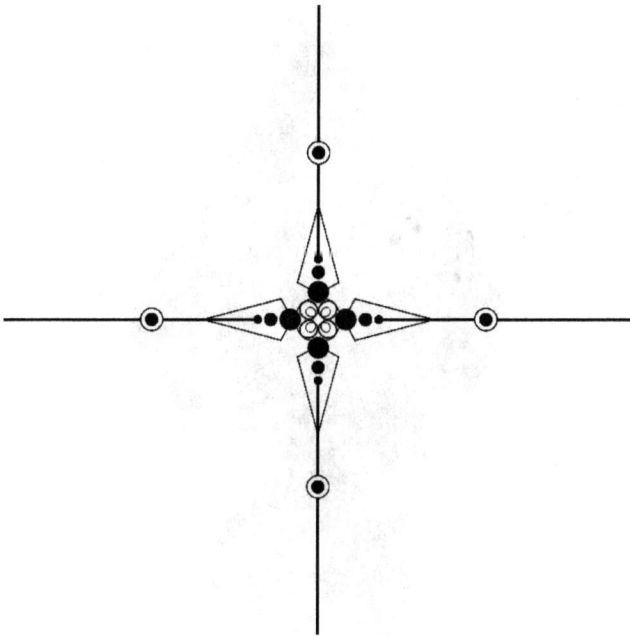

SAGGING

SAGGING

Son, your pants are falling off your
backside.
All can see what you should want to hide
Giving us all an unworthy view
Going up your back, that crease – phheww!
Isn't it sad? What must you think?
No, it's not nice.
In fact, it stinks!
Do you think that this is attractive?
Dirty drawers are no tactic.
You don't attract young ladies of sub-stance
By displaying your under-pants.
Look how you walk, holding on to those pants
Grabbing your crotch
As if in a dance.
It looks so vulgar
So silly
So sad
Pants falling down
It should make you mad.
And what young lady will want to walk with you
With her head held high

While like a duck you waddle by.

And woe to you

As you fill out those applications

As potential employers view

Your unworthy ass-pirations.

Your sagging does prepare you for a destination

As prison walls await your ass-pirations.

For I've been told that it is a state-ment

To tag young men for sexual in-tent.

There are much better ways to show your individuality

Blessed with so much potentiality.

Your mind is a universe of thoughts and dreams

Exercise your gifts, you have the means.

Sagging – it's a phase

But one that damages your productive days.

For with sagging comes no good intent

Bottom line – it certainly won't help you pay your rent.

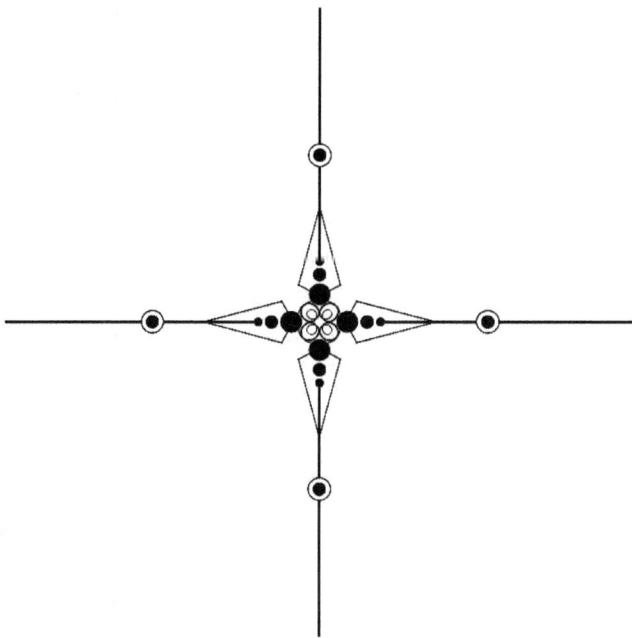

BLACK ON BLACK CRIME

BLACK-ON-BLACK CRIME

Wake up, people
Don't you see
What has happened to you and to me?
A war has been declared.
A war not nation against nation
But a war against ourselves
Against black-on-black relations.

Where did it start
From whence it came?
This hatred we have
This hatred in the name of   BLACKNESS.

To find an answer we must go back.
For 400 years we must track.
To a time when we were royal and free
Free to love ourselves – Free to be
A beautiful people – PEOPLE FREE.

And then an uproar went through our land
As our children were taken
Stolen from our hands.
Shackled and shipped to a foreign land
Stripped of our dignity
We were made to be
Servants to a land
No longer free.

Demeaned, degraded
Forced to bow down
Keeping our eyes
Bowed to the ground
STRIPPED OF OUR HUMANITY
BEATEN DOWN.

But God prevailed.
He made us strong.
Through adversities we survived.
We survived to live on.

And now
At this point in time
Another threat has come
BLACK-ON-BLACK CRIME.

Why has it come to this?
What is the reason
That we have declared
A killing season

ON EACH OTHER
OUR OWN SISTERS AND BROTHERS.

The answer is not simple.
No, it's rather complex.
A conspiracy has developed.
Have minds been vexed?

When we were brought
To this land
Servant to
And hated by the white man.

We were taught
That we were nothing
Not worthy of love
Rewarded when we hurt each other.

DISCOURAGED
WHEN WE LOVED.

As we gained our freedom
Through struggle and pain
The mindsets changed slowly
Self-love was yet to be regained.

It did not help
When we lost access
To the minds of our CHILDREN
Our future – our BEST.

And their minds were shaped to believe
That they were not worthy.
They were evil – not good

THAT WE SHOULD BE SUSPICIOUS
OF THOSE IN OUR OWN NEIGHBORHOODS.

Took all the POWER
Took all the HOPE
Then suppliers introduced suicidal dope.

Put us in projects
Like rats in a cage
To kill each other with powerlessness and rage.

Powerless, hurting, helpless and poor
We turned on each other
'Cause we were not sure
Of an answer to this mixed-up life.

AND OUT OF HOPELESSNESS, FRUSTRATION
AND DESPAIR- A BLACK TAKES ANOTHER BLACK'S LIFE.

But wake up, people
The answer is in you
For GOD is not dead
He values BLACK LIVES too.

He does not want
Our race to die.
He loves us
MANDINKA, BAKONGO AND ASHANTI.

Children keep your heads
LOVE WHO YOU ARE
For one day – not very far
We will rise up, our power we will gain.

WE'LL EMBRACE EACH OTHER
SELF-LOVE WE'LL PROCLAIM.

And BLACK-ON-BLACK CRIME will no longer exist.
For there is no greater love than this
That a BLACK MAN will lay down his life
FOR HIS BROTHER.

NO
EXCUSES

NO EXCUSES

You may live in the projects, yes, it's true.

But the project does not live in you.

Your heart, your soul, your head, your hands

Have been molded and guided by God's plan.

Raised as a child in the way you should go,

From the time of your birth, God's Word we would sow.

You are a blessed child, conceived in love.

Sustained by prayers to our Father above.

So, keep your head up, you must keep your pride

Keep God's Word always by your side.

Keep your eyes on the prize.

For one day you'll rise.

Do not let life get you down

Your final destination is heaven bound.

Rise above the poverty, the violence, the hurt

The vulgarity, discrimination, and yes, the dirt.

Above the backbiting, the fighting, the strife

Rise above all obstacles that shadow your life.

God gave you all He had to give

Gave His only begotten Son so that you could live.

Live indeed your life to the fullest

God only asks that you give Him your best.

Where you live, it matters not.

What matters most is what's in your heart.

Your heart has been filled with love and hope

Not violence, vulgarity, defeat, or dope.

So, do not let the world destroy your dreams.

Your life is the Lord's; lift Him up in all things.

So, son you may live in the projects, yes, it's true.

But the project does not live in you.

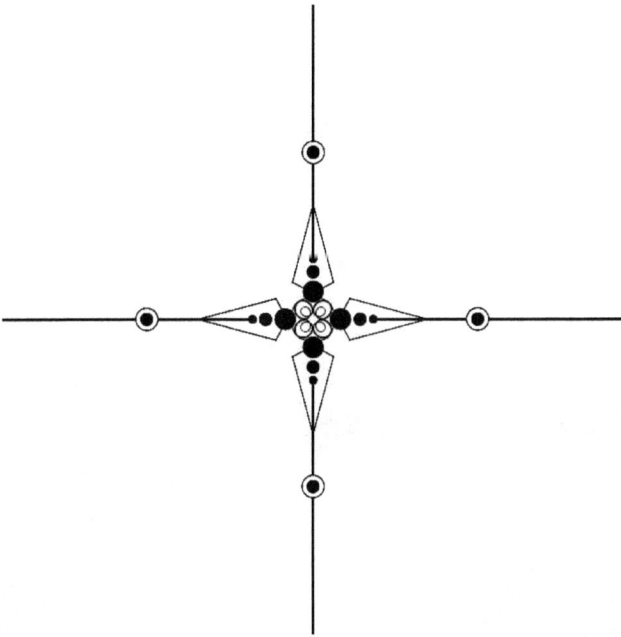

I CAN'T
BREATHE

I CAN'T BREATHE

What prevents you from getting to know me? What have you been taught, what have you been told about people with my skin color? Can't you see that I have two eyes just like you, two ears, two hands, two feet just like you? I bleed the same color blood as you do.

And just like you, I grieve when I lose a loved one. I laugh when I'm happy, cry when I'm sad. I love hard and experience pain.

Never would I look down on someone because they are a different color, live on the other side of town, worship a different God, or love in a different way.

Throughout the years the hurt and pain of being denied the same opportunities as others whose skin is of a different color has been demeaning, debilitating, and defeating.

Because of systemic injustice, I've had to have that talk with my black son and I've had to fall down on my knees when he went out, praying that he would come home.

Respect is due to everyone regardless of race, creed, or color; it's due for humanity's sake, but you look down upon those who are different.

My first breaths in this world signaled my journey here on earth. A journey searching for the answer to why I am relegated to second-class citizenship just because of the amount of melanin in my skin.

Because of this injustice, I CAN'T BREATHE!

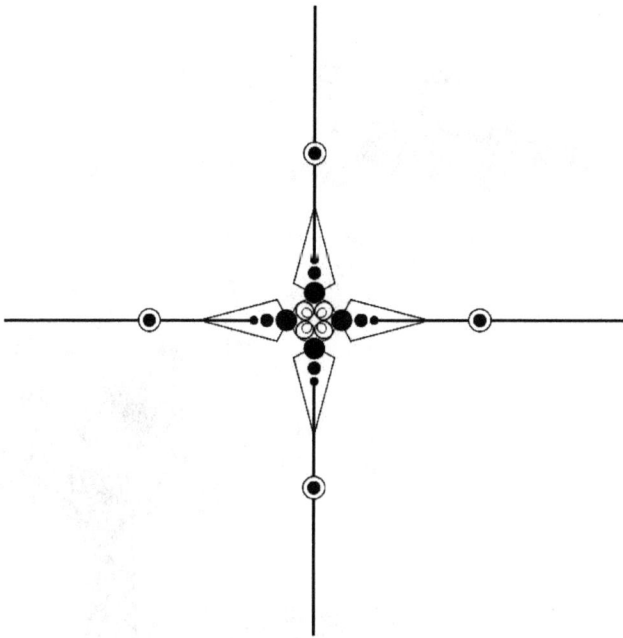

OUT AGAIN

OUT AGAIN

Now I must go out again

Into a world not fit for man

How I long to freely play

Uninhibited in any way.

No thoughts of death

Or dying yet

Just running, hiding, playing.

My friend Andre'

Forgot one day

And carelessly went out to play

As free as a bird he wanted to be

Running, flying, soaring free.

When out from the street there came a sound

And Andre' was spinning, falling down.

His eyes rolled back.

His throat, it trembled

As the neighborhood all assembled.

When out of the crowd came a blood-curdling scream.

Andre's mother cried, "My life, my dream."

As Andre lay in a puddle of blood

My mind with thoughts began to flood

With visions of meadows green and fair

With daffodils, tulips, and butterflies there.

A gentle breeze floats through the air.

The birds sing

The bees fly by

Under the most beautiful clear, blue sky.

The fluffy clouds billow

The sun shines bright

It's always day there, never dark night.

Where children run and romp and play

With no worry of living to see the next day.

Beautiful thoughts of joy, love, and hope

Have replaced those of hunger, killing and dope.

A beautiful place with a radiant glow.

And then all of a sudden, I realize, I know

This is the kind of place where Andre' longed to be.

Anyhow now, he's there, he's made it, he's free

To be the child he wanted to be.

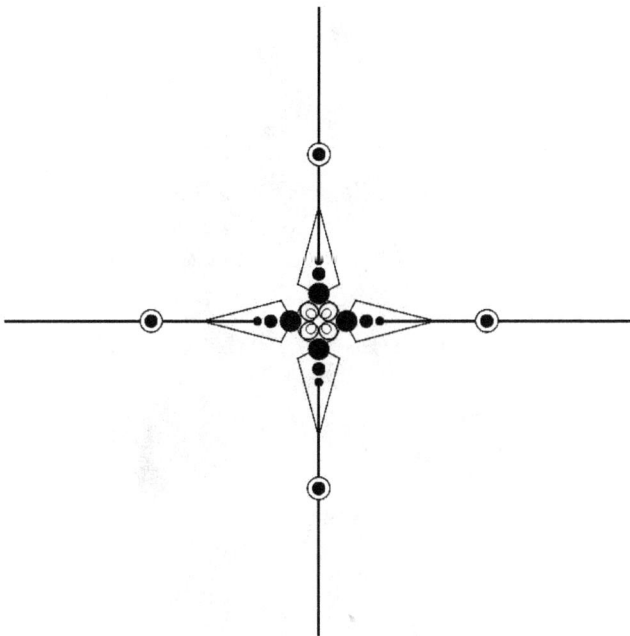

MELVIN'S
DIALOGUE

MELVIN'S DIALOGUE

I had no choice coming into this world the way that I am. You wonder why I have so much rage, why I explode at any given moment without being provoked. My mere existence is provocation. For I did not ask to be. I did not ask to come into a world like this, into a home with so much lack. Existing because of a mere act of copulation.

You wonder why the countenance on my face is always devoid of emotion. 'Cause love, affection, friendship, and peace I have never learned/never experienced. Nobody cares for me. I'm just an occupant of space and time, an object in the way. I'm told quite often how worthless I am. What must I do to be worth something? I know other kids who are "worth something." They look like happy kids too. They're always clean, wear the best clothes and shoes. Their hair is always in place. Their noses aren't running, faces aren't dirty. They don't smell. They always have lunches. Sometimes they'll give some of it to me if I ask.

Kids who are "worth something" have warm houses with their own rooms. They can sleep all night because it's quiet there, no gunshots or sounds of people fighting, glass breaking, cussing. Their toes aren't cold or nibbled on by rats that jump into their beds at night.

They don't have roaches that crawl over their bodies. Kids that are "worth something" can eat at any time of the day they want. They don't have to wait to see if their momma can borrow food stamps to get some bologna and bread. They don't have to eat mayonnaise sandwiches. Kids that are "worth something" know how to put their arms around someone and hug back because they get lots of hugs. Kids who are "worth something" have nicknames like "Precious" and "Pumpkin."

The names I'm called, I get in trouble about when I say them at school. So, teacher, you wonder why I am like I am. Now I hope that you understand. I was brought into this world by way of anger, not love. Crack cocaine throbbed through the veins of the man and woman who conceived me. Is it any wonder that I am the way I am? I want to be "worth something." So teacher, each time that I explode for no reason, each bite, each kick, each scratch is my way of fighting off the demons that occupy my world. Teacher – you just happen to be in the way!

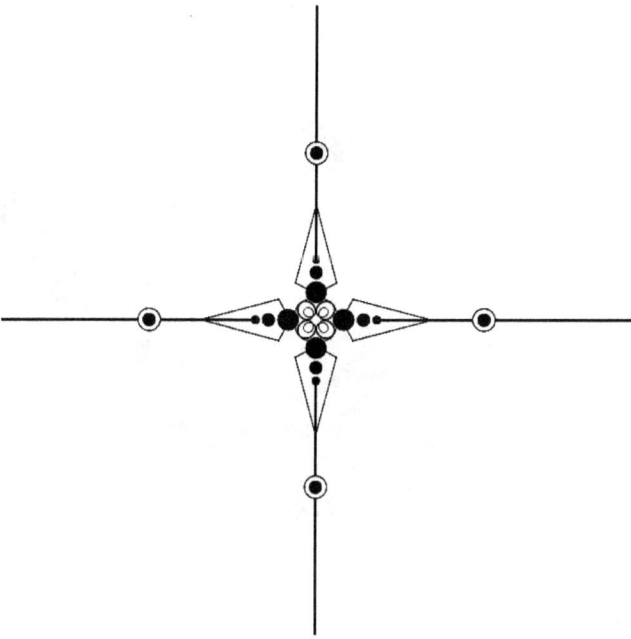

SWEET LITTLE BOY
CHILD

SWEET LITTLE BOY CHILD

Brown eyes fixed on momma as you coo, you gurgle, and you smile.

The sweet countenance on your face has the entire waiting room enthralled.

Smiles of acceptance shine from all faces of all races.

ANGRY BOY CHILD

Brown eyes fixed on momma as you spout filthy vulgarities to everyone in your presence.
The contortions on your face reflect the waiting volcanic eruptions inside your being.

Looks of disdain emanate from all the people around you, From people of all races.

What happened to you between the time you were that sweet, cuddly little boy, so pleased with the world

Now, an angry teenager on the brink of explosion, of eruption?

What led to this drastic change?

Let's check them off.

You grew up in a home where there was so much lack.

You lacked a father because your dad could not get a steady job.

He tried repeatedly only to be denied. His lack of an education didn't help the situation. Suddenly, your dad died, your dad is gone and your single mother is trying to raise you alone. Many days you couldn't go to school because you had to work to help momma to pay the rent and get food for your brothers and sisters. During this time, your mother could not get any social assistance. There is never enough to eat. The lights and phones are often turned off. You often run the streets because mom is working a second low paying job at night.

What are some factors that contributed to this change?
Now you fill in the blanks.

_____   _____

_____   _____

_____   _____

_____   _____

_____   _____

_____   _____

_____   _____

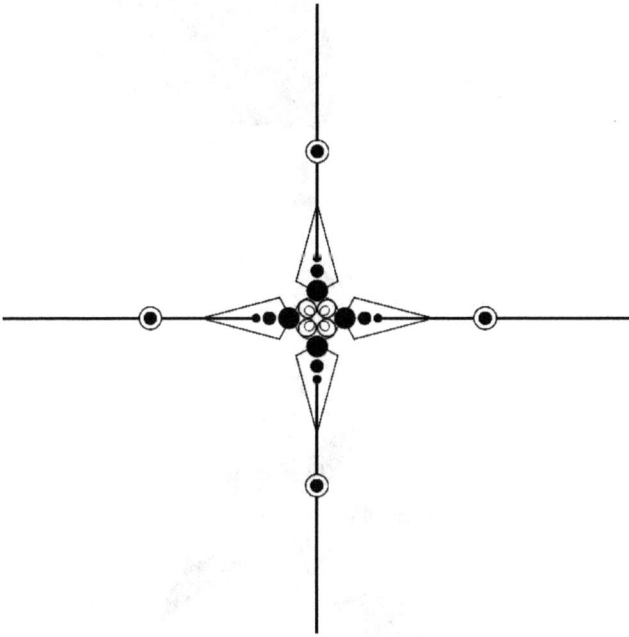

BEWARE OF THE
SEEDS WE PLANT

BEWARE OF THE SEEDS WE PLANT

Do all that you want to do, get your nails done

And don't bother to provide her with wholesome

Activities to nurture her growth.

Do what you want to do, get your pedicure

And don't take the time to help her with her schoolwork.

Watch your football on TV

And never take time to play catch with him.

Buy that fast food

Instead of making nutritious meals to eat.

Sleep in on Sundays

Instead of taking your child to Sunday School.

Be critical instead of encouraging.

Don't take the time to read to your child

Just sit him in front of the TV.

Don't take time to talk to him.

Don't teach him how to tie a tie

Or how to shake a hand and look others in the eye.

Don't teach him how to live on a budget.

Don't attend parent-teacher conferences.

Don't tell your child that you love him.

Continue to cuss him and call him out of his name.

Tell him often that he is good for nothing.

Don't show that you're ever proud of him.

Don't schedule time for her.

Only talk to him when you're hollering at him.

Don't hug her and don't let her know that you care.

Let him come and go as he pleases.

Have no concern about who his friends are

Or what he's doing while locked up in his room.

Just ignore the strange odors in his clothing.

Take his side against those teachers who are "picking on him."

Let him sag, nobody's going to tell your child what to do.

Never mind that in life, he'll have to answer to someone

Or that if he continues on the same path, he'll answer to some prison guard.

Buy her what she wants even when you know it's not good for her.

Allow him to talk to you just any kind of way.

Ignore and don't question him about all that money he has.

Better yet, help him to spend it.

Bail him out time after time with no consequences.

Turn your back when you see him doing wrong.

Follow this recipe – and your child will struggle all his or her life.

Stir in your many excuses and tears.

Prepare for a life filled with many fears.

BEWARE OF THE SEEDS WE PLANT

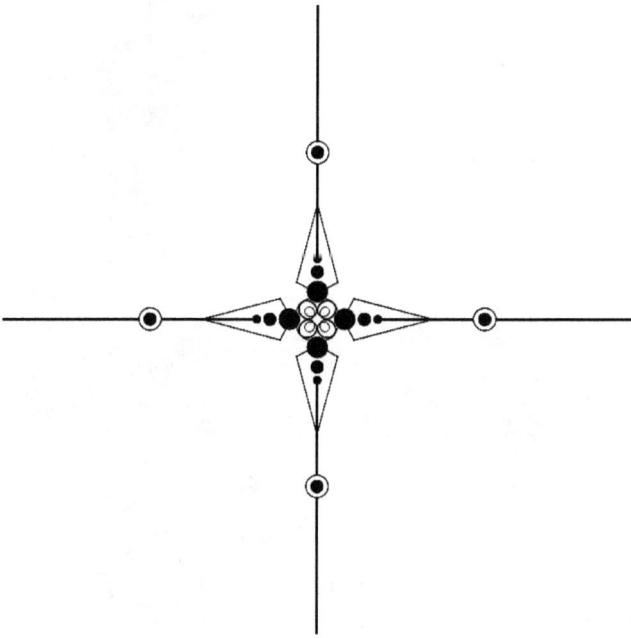

WHERE WE'VE COME FROM

WHERE WE'VE COME FROM

Brought me from a little shack

To a mansion on a hill.

From always being hungry

To always being filled.

Put shoes on my two feet

And clothes on my back.

I'm always in abundance

Never want or lack.

Blessed all my children

Met all their needs.

Even provided for their wants

As they prayed on their knees.

Protected us from our enemies

Traveling to and fro

When trouble came our way

YOU said, "Trouble you've got to go."

When we look back

And see from where we've come

We know we've been blessed

From where we've come from.

WE ARE THE LEADERS OF
TOMORROW

WE ARE THE LEADERS OF TOMORROW

We are the leaders of tomorrow

The future of this world we live in today.

And though this world may be filled with trouble and sorrow

It will not always be that way.

Our ancestors always took the time

To lift us up in prayer.

And we prevailed because God made us strong.

So, God's strength as tomorrow's leaders we'll share.

Our forefathers prayed for their children's futures

And through adversities they survived.

So, we too must lift God up

As toward heaven's gates we strive.

If our future is to ever be bright

Families must go back to those OLD days.

When prayers went up and blessings came down

Lighting their children's pathways.

So, lift God up in everything you do

He'll be with us for always.

Then God-fearing leaders, we will be too

Because we'll be leaders who prayed.

HAD I
KNOWN

HAD I KNOWN

Had I known that you'd leave me
I would have hugged you more often
I would have shared more of my time,
I would have loved you more dearly
Made all of your time, mine.
I would have cherished each moment
As new morning dew,
Counted all of our blessings
As we shared each other's views.
Had I known that you would leave me
I would have explored every door.
Your laughter, your joys, your disappointments
I would have given so much more.
I would have given much more generously
Made your wishes, my commands
Faced each day with renewed commitment
Talking to you with prayer-clasped hands.
Had I known that you would leave,
I would have cherished every day,
As I looked deeply into your eyes
Quietly praying for you to stay.
But it was not to be

As death between us stood
To take you, my love, away from me
Separating as only death could.
Had I known that you would leave me
I would have appreciated you more
I would have savored every moment
Before you entered heaven's door.

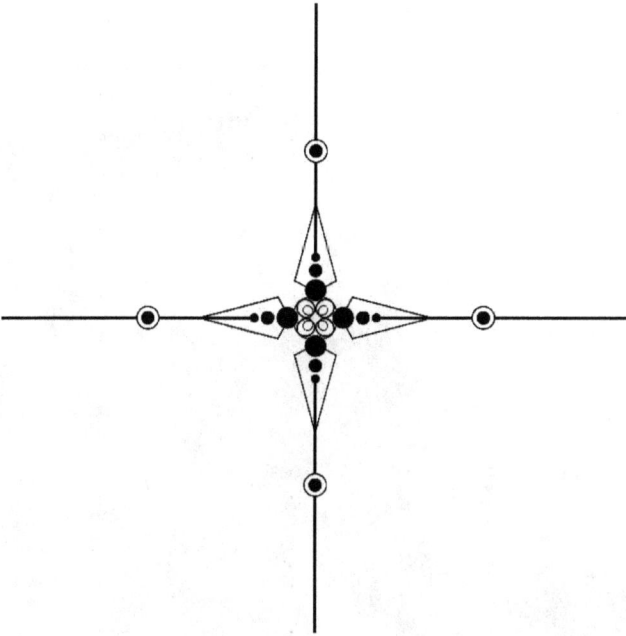

INDEPENDENCE
DAY

INDEPENDENCE DAY

(For Victims of Domestic Battery)

The legal term is domestic battery

A fancy term for him whipping your head.

And scarring and battering your body

Until you wished that you were dead.

You do this because you say you love me?

What type of foolishness is that?

Foolish enough that I believed it

But your heart showed only lack.

When we first met you were oh so smooth

There was never enough time with you.

Your love for me you would constantly prove

In all that you would say and do.

But suddenly things started to change

I seemed to do nothing right.

As your controlling ways became so strange

That just visiting my friends led to fights.

You started screening my phone calls

You followed me home and to work.

Between me and my friends you put up walls

Whatever I did, to you was like dirt.

You made me question who I am

And what I wanted to be.

You belittled me in front of my friends

And hurt the very inside of me.

With each day of our relationship

A little piece of me died.

All my dreams, ambitions, hopes, desires

Left my body with each tear that I cried.

You told me that I could never leave you

That I could never leave your side.

For on that day you would send me roses.

Because it would be that day that I died.

You threatened my children, my family

And I've lived in fear of this.

But be it known by you today

Listen carefully, this message don't miss.

I am no longer afraid of you

I can make it on my own.

God protects me through and through

To move my life along.

All that I must do

Is to take that very first step.

With love and support that He's given

I'll survive and by His love, I'll be kept.

And so, I say this to my sisters all

This message is for each of you.

Don't be a victim; to abuse don't fall

See your worth through and through.

Never let anyone devalue your worth

You are a Queen and even more.

One day someone will see your heart

And will love you to your deepest core.

You do not have to settle

Just to say to your best friend,

I don't know about you

But honey, "I've got a man."

Sisters shout your declarations

Lift your voices loud and say,

I am free of this man's abuse

IT'S MY INDEPENDENCE DAY!

AM I NOT
ENOUGH

AM I NOT ENOUGH?

My hips are far from perfect but they carried our pride.

My breasts no longer round and firm, no smoothness in my stride

 I have suckled our little ones and my beauty is long gone.

My complexion blotched and drab, with no longer an even tone

My face once round and plumb is now filled with fine lines

The bags beneath my eyes signal the hard times

My hair is no longer silky the black hues replaced by grey

My eyes have lost their clearness they're cloudy in the light of day

My voice no longer smooth and sensual as haughtily I speak

My teeth no longer pearly white my lips so thin and weak

Time has taken a toll on this old body of mine

But my mind and heart remain the same, unchanged over time

My love and devotion to my family is still more than enough

Enough to last for a lifetime!

FAITH, HOPE AND
LOVE

FAITH, HOPE AND LOVE

These three, but the greatest of these is love.

Could not have made it

To this point in my life

Without these three.

Without faith could not move forward

My feet would be bolted to the ground.

Unable to move because of the unknown

Holding back due to fear.

Without hope, I could not dream

My mind would be in bondage.

I would not know what could be.

As I wallowed in pity each day.

Without love, I would not live

No joy would I ever know

No peace would my heart experience

As these are the product of love.

Faith, Hope and Love

These three, but the greatest of these is Love.

MORNING
DEW

MORNING DEW

Glistening, sparkling like diamonds do
Caressing the short-cropped blades of grass
But it's not diamonds, it's morning dew
Signaling the morning's dawn at last.

Tiny twinkling mounds sparkling on the lawn
As butterflies and ladybugs fly by
Carrying droplets of moisture into the dawn
Under the most beautiful clear blue sky.
So delicate the touch of morning dew
As it flutters down to the earth
Kissing each object with its crystal hue
Welcoming the dawning of the day's birth.

Observe as it blankets the manicured lawns
Like stars in the Milky Way
Blinking like rays streaming from the sun
Announcing this brand-new day.

Oh, how God's earth eagerly awaits
The arrival of this morning dew
As drinks from His overflowing fountain make

The treasured cycle of life anew.

God's gift of morning dew
Awakens all that is below.
It saturates the land as only He can do
While in our hearts His love He does sow!

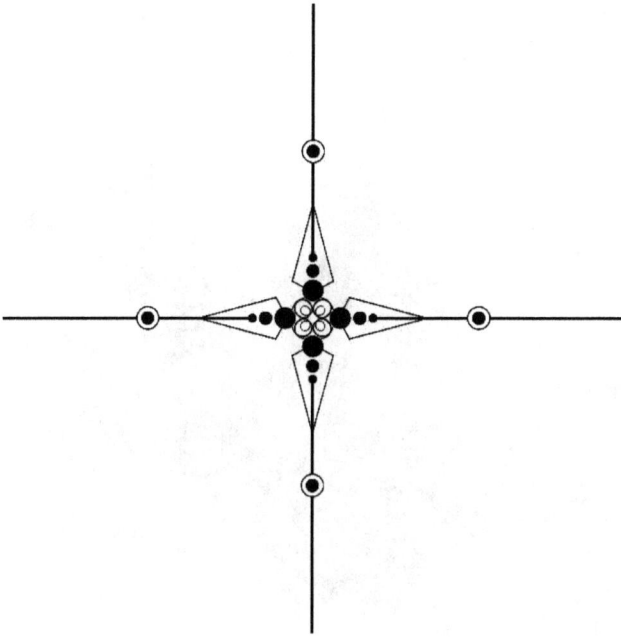

SHOUT YOUR WIG
OFF

SHOUT YOUR WIG OFF

Sister Johnson rocked the aisles today

Praising God in her own way.

Jumping and shouting and running around

Till her curly grey wig finally hit the ground.

Deacon Smith tried to hold her

But to no avail.

As she bumped into Usher Jones

And knocked her over the rail.

All the children snickered

As she would jump and shout

From one end of the pew

Then on the other end out.

She shouted and jumped so hard

She knocked over the offering table.

Brother Brown, who's 99, jumped out of the way

Even though he's disabled.

(I've never seen him move quite that fast).

But he wasn't gonna be a part of that crash.

She had so much praise and joy, and why do you ask?

'Cause on that day, her son gave his life to Christ

And in God's glory she basked.

DON'T LET THE GOLIATHS IN YOUR LIFE
IN YOUR LIFE
DISTURB YOU

DON'T LET THE GOLIATHS IN YOUR LIFE DISTURB YOU

This morning the pastor said, "Don't let the Goliaths in your life disturb you." We all know the story of David and Goliath found in the book of 1 Samuel in the Bible.

David was a shepherd boy, the eighth son of Jesse. David slew a giant with a slingshot, a rock, and the power of God.

Goliath was the Philistines' greatest weapon, a giant over nine feet tall. David, a humble shepherd boy, killed this giant because Goliath had rebuked and mocked his God. God rewarded David by choosing him as Israel's next king.

Each one of us have faced Goliaths in our lives. From the time we were born, we have faced problems that seemed like giants. But just like David, we must trust God, depend on His Word, and He will bring us through. Below are some of the problems of this world faced by so many, followed by scripture to inspire, guide and direct. Please pray and meditate on these scriptures and others and experience the power of God!

PLEASE PRAY FOR...

The baby born to crack-addicted parents whose blood coursed with the illicit drug...

"Before I formed you in the womb I knew you, before you were born I set you apart." (Jeremiah 1:5 New International Version)

"Let us thank the God and Father of our Lord Jesus Christ. It was through his loving kindness that we were born again to a new life and have a hope that never dies. This hope is ours because Jesus was raised from the dead." (1 Peter 1:3 New Life Version)

The mother who sells her body for her next fix...

"Do you not know that your bodies are temples of the Holy Spirit, who is in you, whom you have received from God? You are not your own; you were bought with a price. Therefore, glorify God in your body, and in your spirit, which are God's." (1 Corinthians 6:19 NIV)

The adolescent with self-esteem problems because she has no one in her life who loves her or cares for her needs...

"Never will I leave you; never will I forsake you." (Hebrews 13:5 NIV)

"And my God will meet all your needs according to the riches of his glory in Christ Jesus." (Philippians 4:19 NIV)

The young teen, pregnant and afraid...

"For I am the LORD your God who takes hold of your right hand and says to you, Do not fear: I will help you." (Isaiah 41:13 NIV)

The teenage girl who is abused by her father with the knowledge of abuse by her mother and the feeling of no way out...

"The LORD is good, a refuge in times of trouble. He cares for those who trust in Him." (Nahum 1:7 NIV)

The young adult who can't find a job and is tempted to support himself by selling drugs…

"Trust in the LORD and do good. Then you will live safely in the land and prosper." (Psalm 37:33 New Living Translation)

The young wife who is dependent upon a man who constantly degrades, puts down and verbally and physically abuses her…

"The LORD will grant that the enemies who rise up against you will be defeated before you. They will come at you from one direction but flee from you in seven." (Deuteronomy 28:7 NIV)

The young father who is struggling to raise his family, but who has a wife who is only interested in acquiring things and enjoying the pleasures of life…

"I will show you and teach you in the way you should go. I will tell you what to do with my eye upon you." (Psalm 32:8 New Life Version)

The faithful employee who tries so hard every day to do his best, only to be berated sabotaged, mocked, and put down by his fellow employees and employer…

"Thou shalt have a perfect and just weight, a perfect and just measure shalt thou have that thy days may be lengthened in the land which the LORD thy God giveth thee. For all that do such things, and all that do unrighteously, are an abomination unto the LORD thy God." (Deuteronomy 25:15–16)

The honest corporate executive who brings integrity to his job only to be ridiculed because of his honesty...

"Those who walk righteously and speak what is right, who reject gain from extortion and keep their hands from accepting bribes, who stop their ears against plots of murder and shut their eyes against contemplating evil—they are the ones who will dwell on the heights, whose refuge will be the mountain fortress. Their bread will be supplied, and water will not fail them." (Isaiah 33:15–16 NIV)

The teacher who faces students every day who have built up walls around themselves daring her to try to teach them...

"Do not let yourselves get tired of doing good. If we do not give up, we will get what is coming to us at the right time." (Galatians 6:9 NLV)

The grandmother raising her grandchildren because their parents are missing in action or AWOL...

"My body and my heart may grow weak, but God is the strength of my heart and all I need forever." (Psalm 73:26 NLV)

"For with God nothing shall be impossible." (Luke 1:37)

The families faced with unemployment wondering if there will be food for the next meal...

"He will respond to the prayer of the destitute; he will not despise their plea." (Psalm 102:17 NIV)

"But He lifts those in need out of their troubles, He makes their families grow like flocks." (Psalm 107:41 NLV)

He replied, "Because you have so little faith. Truly I tell you if you have faith as small as a mustard seed, you can say to this mountain, 'Move from here to there,' and it will move. Nothing will be impossible for you." (Matthew 17:20 NIV)

The homeless man or woman who is vulnerable to not only the outside elements, but to those with criminal intent...

"Even if you are driven to the ends of the earth, the Lord your God will gather you and bring you back." (Deuteronomy 30:4 NLV)

"The angel of the Lord stays close around those who fear Him, and He takes them out of trouble." (Psalm 34:7 NLV)

"Because you have made the Lord your safe place, and the Most High the place where you live, nothing will hurt you. No trouble will come near your tent." (Psalm 91:9–10 NLV)

Those with a mental disease that takes a toll on their reality...

"In peace I will lie down and sleep, for you alone, LORD, make me dwell in safety." (Psalm 4:8 NIV)
"When you lie down, you will not be afraid; when you lie down, your sleep will be sweet." (Proverbs 3:24 NIV)

"The Lord will keep you from all harm—he will watch over your life; the Lord will watch over your coming and going both now and forevermore." (Psalm 121:7–8 NIV)

The drug abusers who crave their drugs more than life itself...

"My flesh and my heart may fail, but God is the strength of my heart and my portion forever." (Psalm 73:26 NIV)

"But God will redeem me from the realm of the dead; he will surely take me to himself." (Psalm 49:15 NIV)

"So then Christian brothers, we are not to do what our sinful old selves want us to do. If you do what your sinful old selves want you to do, you will die in sin. But if, through the power of the Holy Spirit, you destroy those actions to which the body can be led, you will have life." (Romans 8:12–13 NLV)

The senior citizen abandoned by her children and left to the mercy of the system...

"Know then that the Lord your God is God, the faithful God. He keeps His promise and shows His loving-kindness to those who love Him and keep his Laws, even to a thousand family groups in the future." (Deuteronomy 7:9 NLV)

"The mountains may be taken away and the hills may shake, but my loving-kindness will not be taken from you. And my agreement of peace will not be shaken," says the Lord who has loving pity on you. (Isaiah 54:10 NLV)

The man or woman discriminated against because of the color of their skin, their religion, immigration status, gender, or socio-economic status...

"But now the Lord who made you, O Jacob, and He Who made you, O Israel, says 'Do not be afraid. For I have bought you and made you free, I have called you by name. You are mine!'" (Isaiah 43:1 NLV)

"He will cover you with His feathers, and under his wings you will find refuge; his faithfulness will be your shield and rampart. You will not fear the terror of night, nor the arrow that flies by day, nor the pestilence that stalks in the darkness, nor the plague that destroys at midday." (Psalm 91:4–6 NIV)

"The Lord is my light and my salvation-whom shall I fear? The Lord is the stronghold of my life-of whom shall I be afraid? When the wicked advance against me to devour me, it is my enemies and my foes who will stumble and fall. Though an army besiege me, my heart will not fear; though war break out against me even then I will be confident."(Psalm 27:1–3 NIV)

That person who watches a loved one battle a dreaded disease…

"No, in all these things we are more than conquerors through him who loved us."(Romans 8:37 NIV)
"But the God of all grace, who has called us unto his eternal glory by Christ Jesus, after that ye have suffered a while, make you perfect, stablish, strengthen, settle you." (1 Peter 5:10)

The pastor with a church congregation that chooses not to hear him as he preaches the Word…

96

"Most assuredly, I say to you, he who believes in Me, the works that I do, he will do also; and greater works than these he will do, because I go to My Father." (John 12:12 New King James Version)

"The Spirit of the LORD is on me, because he has anointed me to proclaim good news to the poor. He has sent me to proclaim freedom for the prisoners and recovery of sight for the blind, to set the oppressed free, to proclaim the year of the Lord's favor." (Luke 4:18–20 NIV)

"If you remain in me and my words remain in you, ask whatever you wish, and it will be done for you." (John 15:7 NIV)

That person addicted to pornography…

"Be diligent to present yourself approved to God, a worker who does not need to be ashamed, rightly dividing the word of truth." (2 Timothy 2:15 NKJV)

"Bless the Lord, O my soul, and forget not all His benefits, Who forgives all your iniquities, Who heals all your diseases, Who redeems your life from destruction, Who crowns you with lovingkindness and tender mercies." (Psalm 103:2–4 NKJV)
"And be not conformed to this world; but be ye transformed by the renewing of your mind, that ye may prove what is that good, and acceptable and perfect will of God." (Romans 12:2)

That student who needs financial aid so that he can be the first in his family to go to college…

"And my God will meet all your needs according to the riches of his glory in Christ Jesus." (Philippians 4:19 NIV)

"If you abide in Me, and My word abide in you, you will ask what you desire, and it shall be done for you." (John 15:7 NKJV)

That person who is lonely and friendless...

"Fear not, for I am with you: Be not dismayed for I am your God. I will strengthen you, yes, I will help you, I will uphold you with My righteous right hand." (Isaiah 41:10 NKJV)

"A friend loveth at all times, and a brother is born for adversity." (Proverbs 17:17)

"A merry heart doeth good like a medicine; but a broken spirit drieth the bones." (Proverbs 17:22 NIV)

"They helped every one his neighbor; and every one said to his brother, Be of good courage." (Isaiah 41:6)

That person who does all that he or she can but is still not appreciated...

"Therefore be patient, brethren, until the coming of the Lord. See how the farmer waits for the precious fruit of the earth, waiting patiently for it until it receives the early and latter rain. You also be patient. Establish your hearts, for the coming of the Lord is at hand." (James 5:7–8 NKJV)
"Persecuted, but not abandoned; struck down, but not destroyed." (2 Corinthians 4:9 NIV)

"Let us hold fast the profession of our faith without wavering; (for he is faithful that promised)." (Hebrews 10:23)

That single mother working two jobs trying to feed the kids, pay the rent and clothe her children...

"No, in all things we are more than conquerors through him who loved us." (Romans 8:37 NIV)

"Therefore, I say, whatever things you ask when you pray, believe that you receive them, and you will have them." (Mark 11:24 NKJV)

"If you abide in Me, and My Words abide in you, you will ask what you desire, and it shall be done for you." (John 15:7 NKJV)

That person rejected by his or her family...

"Though my father and mother forsake me, the Lord will receive me." (Psalm 27:10 NIV)

"The Lord is close to the brokenhearted, and saves those who are crushed in spirit." (Psalm 34:18 NIV)

That young girl caught up in the sex trade...
"My body and my heart may grow weak, but God is my strength of my heart and all I need forever." (Psalm 73:26 NLV)

"For He has not turned away from the suffering of the one in pain or trouble. He has not hidden His face from him. But He has heard his cry for help." (Psalm 22:34 NLV)

"Call unto me and I will answer thee, and shew thee great and mighty things, which thou knowest not." (Jeremiah 33:3)

That mother or father whose child is deployed across the seas at a time when war seems imminent...

"Peace I leave with you. My peace I give to you. I do not give to you as the world gives. Do not let your hearts be troubled and do not be afraid." (John 14:27 NIV)

"I pray that the God who gives hope will fill you with much joy and peace while you trust in him. Then your hope will overflow by the power of the Holy Spirit." (Romans 15:13 New Century Version)

That child who is struggling because of a disability and the mom who needs support...

"He gives strength to the weak. He gives power to him who has little strength." (Isaiah 40:29 NLV)

"Be strong. Be strong in heart, all you who hope in the Lord." (Psalm 31:24 NLV)

"I am the good shepherd: the good shepherd giveth his life for the sheep." (John 10:11)

"The Lord is my shepherd; I shall not want. He maketh me to lie down in green pastures: he leadeth me besides the still waters. He restoreth my soul: he leadeth me in the paths of righteousness for His name sake. Yea though I walk through the valley of the shadow of death, I will fear no evil: for thou art with me; thy rod and thy staff they comfort me." (Psalm 23:1–4)

That man, woman, boy or girl searching for his or her identity...

"Thou wilt keep him in perfect peace, whose mind is stayed on thee: because he trusteth in thee." (Isaiah 26:3)

"Nay, in all these things we are more than conquerors through him that loved us." (Romans 8:37)

"We are troubled on every side, yet not distressed; we are perplexed, but not in despair; Persecuted, but not forsaken; cast down, but not destroyed; Always bearing about in the body the dying of the Lord Jesus, that the life also of Jesus might be manifest in our body." (2 Corinthians 4:8–10)

That person who is imprisoned mentally and/or physically...

"Therefore if any man be in Christ, he is a new creature; old things are passed away; behold, all things are become new." (2 Corinthians 5:17)

"Being born again, not of corruptible seed, but of incorruptible, by the Word of God, which liveth and abideth forever." (1 Peter 1:23)

"God makes a home for those who are alone. He leads men out of prison into happiness and wellbeing. But those who fight against Him live in an empty desert." (Psalm 68:6 NLV)

"He brought them out of darkness and the shadow of death. And He broke their chains." (Psalm 107:14 NLV)

"But then I will bring health and healing to the people there. I will heal them and let them enjoy great peace and safety." (Jeremiah 33:6 NCV)

That mother who cries for her son or daughter...

"Weeping may endure for a night, but joy comes in the morning." (Psalm 30:5 NKJV)

"Bring up a child by teaching him the way he should go, and when he is old he will not turn away from it." (Proverbs 22:6 NLV)

"He healeth the broken in heart, and bindeth up their wounds." (Psalm 147:3)

That gang member who wants out...

"Do not conform yourselves to the standards of this world, but let God transform you inwardly by a complete change of your mind. Then you will be able to know the will of God—what is good and is pleasing to him and is perfect." (Romans 12:2 Good News Translation)

"Be not overcome of evil but overcome evil with good." (Romans 12:21)

"The Lord is my light and my salvation—whom shall I fear? The LORD is the stronghold of my life—of whom shall I be afraid?" (Psalm 27:1 NIV)

"For in the day of trouble he will keep me safe in his dwelling; he will hide me in the shelter of his sacred tent and set me high upon a rock." (Psalm 27:5 NIV)

"The angel of the LORD encampeth round about them that fear Him, and delivereth them." (Psalm 34:7)

"Yea, though I walk through the valley of the shadow of death, I will fear no evil: for though art with me; thy rod and thy staff they comfort me." (Psalm 23:4)

That child who is being bullied in school...

"Fear though not; for I am with thee; be not dismayed; for I am thy God; I will strengthen thee, yea, I will help thee; yea, I will uphold thee with the right hand of my righteousness." (Isaiah 41:10)

"Come unto me, all ye that labour and are heavy laden, and I will give you rest." (Matthew 11:28)

That person who is searching and searching for a job...

"And this is the confidence that we have in Him, that, if we ask anything according to His will, He heareth us; And if we know that He hears us, whatsoever we ask, we know that we have the petitions that we desired of Him." (1 John 5:14–15)

"For with God, nothing shall be impossible." (Luke 1:37)

"But seek ye first the kingdom of God, and His righteous, and all these things shall be added unto you." (Matthew 6:33)

Those imprisoned by hate, anger, jealousy, and fear...

"I will both lay me down in peace, and sleep: for thou, Lord, only makest me dwell in safety." (Psalm 4:8)

"The LORD himself goes before you and will be with you; he will never leave you nor forsake you. Do not be afraid; do not be discouraged."
(Deuteronomy 31:6 NIV)

"I will lift up mine eyes unto the hills, from whence cometh my help. My help cometh from the Lord, which made heaven and earth."
(Psalm 121:1–2)

Those seeking peace...

"Peace I leave with you; my peace I give you. I do not give to you as the world gives. Do not let your hearts be troubled and do not be afraid." (John 14:27 NIV)
"Let the peace of Christ rule in your hearts, since as members of one body you were called to peace. And be thankful." (Colossians 3:15 NIV)

"For to be carnally minded is death; but to be spiritually minded is life and peace."(Romans 8:6)

We all have Goliaths in our lives. Don't let the Goliaths in your life disturb you! Trust and depend on God and His Word and He will answer your prayers.

Read your Bible, study and pray. God will bring you through. **BE ENCOURAGED!**

www.ingramcontent.com/pod-product-compliance
Lightning Source LLC
Chambersburg PA
CBHW060119050426
42448CB00010B/1953